I. M. PEI

I. M. PEI

Aileen Reid

Crescent Books
New York/Avenel, New Jersey

This 1995 edition published by Crescent Books distributed by Random House Value Publishing Inc., 40 Englehard Avenue Avenel, New Jersey 07001

Random House New York · Toronto · London · Sydney · Auckland

Produced by Brompton Books Corporation 15 Sherwood Place, Greenwich, CT 06830

ISBN 0-517-10299-4

8 7 6 5 4 3 2 1

Printed and bound in China

PAGE 1: Bank of China, interior.

PAGE 2: Creative Artists' Agency, atrium.

PAGES 4-5: The Bank of China dominating the Hong Kong skyline.

CONTENTS

Introduction   6

The Development of an Architect, 1950-66   24

Acclaim in America, 1966-77   46

An International Reputation, 1978-94   74

The Louvre, Phases I-III, 1988-93   106

Acknowledgments   112

Introduction

Architects are not popular. When Prince Charles made his famous speech to the Royal Institute of British Architecture (RIBA), describing Ahrends, Burton and Koralek's proposed extension to London's National Gallery as a 'carbuncle on the face of a much-loved friend', he stuck a chord with the public. The architects had finally been rumbled, and by a member of the Royal Family, no less. The Prince's reaction to the Modernist design for the National Gallery extension, and the effect that his damning words had on the Gallery's trustees in convincing them to choose a safe, classicizing design for the prominent Trafalgar Square site, provide a sharp and telling contrast to the way I. M. Pei's no less modern, even more unusual 'pyramid' additions to the Louvre Museum in Paris have been received.

There are various reasons for the difference in reception, which will be discussed in the chapter on the Louvre, but one result of the popularity of the pyramids has been to make a household name of I. M. Pei. If one were to stop people in the street in New York, London, Paris and Hong Kong and ask them to name *living* architects, I. M. Pei's is probably the only name that would come up in each. This is all the more remarkable in that this international reputation has only really been established since I. M. Pei reached his seventies.

Although he is now often described as an American architect, Ieoh Ming Pei only arrived in the United States as a student in the mid-1930s, and until the late 1940s still expected to return to China. He was born on 26 April 1917 in Suzhou, a city to the north-west of Shanghai, where his family had been settled for 600 years. His father, Tsuyee Pei, was an official for the Bank of China, for which he worked in Beijing, Shanghai, Hong Kong and Guangzhou. The family had to leave the last rather hurredly in 1918 because of civil unrest, but by 1927 Tsuyee Pei was manager of the Bank of China's headquarters in Shanghai.

Shanghai in the 1920s and 1930s was a liberal and westernized city, attracting much American and European business. I. M. Pei was educated by Protestant missionaries at St John's School. The lessons were in Chinese, though they read the Bible and some Dickens in English. Although Tsuyee Pei had made many British contacts from the years he worked in Hong Kong, and strongly urged his son to study in England, the young I. M. Pei dreamed only of the America that he had seen in Shanghai's movie theaters. He reluctantly agreed to sit the examinations for entrance to Oxford University, but only on the condition that if he passed he could then make up his own mind about where to study.

The fact that Oxford has never had a School of Architecture was, surprisingly, not the reason for Pei's turning down his offer of a place there. He did not have a burning ambition to be an architect and has said that he was as likely to become a doctor or a lawyer. What swung it for him is supposed to have been seeing the 23-story Park Hotel, a verit-

LEFT: I. M. Pei in front of his famous glass pyramid in the main courtyard of the Louvre Museum, the Cour Napoléon, during construction of the vast underground space which he designed to give easy access to every part of the museum.

ABOVE RIGHT: The formal reopening of the Cour Napoléon on 3 July 1988, the eve of Bastille Day, when the pyramid was lit for the first time.

able skyscraper in pre-war Chinese terms, being built in Shanghai. The other factor was the tempting descriptions of the architecture course at the University of Pennsylvania, and it was there he headed. Tempting though the prospectus may have been, Pei soon found the atmosphere at Penn stifling. Far from being a hotbed of Modernism, the School favored the long-established Beaux-Arts approach, which stressed the primacy of Greek and Roman buildings and philosophy, and of skill in drawing arrived at through hours spent copying from casts of classical statues. Pei felt he could never compete with students who had received their schooling in the West and had developed these skills over many years, so in fall 1935 he transferred to the engineering course at MIT.

The dean of MIT's architecture school, William Emerson, recognized what a waste of talent it would be if Pei abandoned architecture and, after a lot of persuasion, Pei returned to his original subject. Not that MIT was at the cutting edge of architectural teaching; Pei later diplomatically admitted that what he gained most from his time there was a solid grounding in structural engineering. But he was an outstanding student and won several honors, including the American Institute of Architects' medal.

While at MIT Pei met Eileen Loo, another Chinese student who had just arrived in the US to study They were married in

1942 and it was partly through Eileen's involvement with Harvard – as a graduate student of landscape architecture – that Pei came to make the most significant move of his architectural education. With the prospect of returning to a China torn by war looking ever more remote, Pei enrolled in December 1942 at Harvard's Graduate School of Design.

Modernism in the US and at Harvard were virtually one and the same thing in the early 1940s. This was due to the arrival there in 1937 of Walter Gropius and Marcel Breuer from the Bauhaus, founded in Germany in 1919 and forced to close by the Nazis in 1933. Pei had initially been attracted by the more expressive Modernism of Le Corbusier, but he was intoxicated by Gropius's Bauhaus philosophy of 'total design' and by the truly integrated teamwork that it required. Pei flourished at Harvard and was valued also as an inspiring and patient teacher.

By 1948 Pei was over 30, had a wife and baby to support, and had never had a 'real' architectural job. It is in this light that one must see what seems his rather odd decision to team up with the flamboyant New York property developer William Zeckendorf, who had recently taken over the firm of Webb & Knapp. They made an odd couple, the huge, brash Jewish New Yorker and the small fastidious Pei, fresh from Boston. But apart from the economic necessities, Pei was impressed by Zeckendorf's drive and vision. Zeckendorf had

LEFT: The young Pei (third from left, front row) with other MIT architecture students, in March 1936.

BELOW LEFT: Pei in 1940, from the *MIT Yearbook*.

BELOW RIGHT: Walter Gropius, former director of the Bauhaus, with whom Pei studied at Harvard.

BELOW FAR RIGHT: Pei's first design for Webb & Knapp was this Modernist cylinder, intended for a site on New York's East River, but not built.

decided there was no reason why a property developer should not be a twentieth-century Lorenzo de' Medici in terms of architectural patronage. When Pei joined Webb & Knapp, Zeckendorf had recently played a part in the United Nations' decision to relocate their headquarters to New York, by selling them a huge tract of land he had acquired for development in east Manhattan.

Much of Zeckendorf's development work, however, was in low-cost housing, for which government funds were available to house returning servicemen. It was for another site on the East River that Pei did his first design for Webb & Knapp, a helical high-rise cylinder of one-bedroom apartments. Not only did it look novel, but it was also flexibly planned, allowing occupants to take over or relinquish other units within the building as their families grew or contracted. It was too novel, however, for even Zeckendorf to build. Zeckendorf's grand schemes had yet to get off the ground, and in the meantime Pei did his first realized project, the 1950 headquarters building for Gulf Oil in Atlanta. Although Pei now denigrates much of his early work, the Gulf Oil building, while a simple Modernist box design, already displayed his trademarks of quality build and fine detailing.

By 1951 Zeckendorf had entrusted Pei with the first of the large-scale planning projects that were to occupy them both for the rest of the decade. This was for a 125-acre shopping center on Roosevelt Field, outside New York, from which Charles Lindbergh had begun his epoch-making flight in 1927. Designed to make the new experience of mall shopping as untiring as possible, Roosevelt Field concentrated the shops in the center, surrounded by parking lots connected by cloverleaf ramps and – a real novelty in 1951 – brick kiosks for drive-in banking.

By this time Pei had taken on, as an assistant at Webb & Knapp, Henry Cobb, who remains with him today as senior partner, and together they undertook a more personal project in the remodeling of Webb & Knapp's Madison Avenue office. Although part of the reconstruction was within the existing building, the most striking feature was Pei's addition of a circular penthouse office for Zeckendorf with floor-to-ceiling glass windows, quite something in austerity-era New York.

Most of Pei's work at Webb & Knapp, however, consisted of redevelopment. It is hard now to imagine Pei as an accomplice of the great operator Zeckendorf, flying back and forth across the country 'casing' cities from the air, calling up and fêting the great and the good in 'targeted' areas, and buttering up the local press. But that seems to have been how it worked. The first project after Roosevelt Field was the Mile High Center and Courthouse Square in Denver, begun in 1952. Although the opportunities for design innovation here were limited, Pei enlivened what is a standard Modernist tower with a delicate, almost basketweave pattern on the facade of grays and whites.

The next project Zeckendorf started, had it been completed according to Pei's plan, would have been the largest redevelopment in the United States to that date. It was designed to rehabilitate 500 acres of south-west Washington DC, creating a 300ft-wide mall all the way from the Smithsonian Institution to the Potomac River, and including a mix of cultural and office facilities. For the first time, however, Pei was to experience the debilitating effects of bureaucratic foot-dragging, financial stringency and municipal in-fighting, and by 1959 the plan had become a compromise. And it

was certainly not the last time Pei experienced such disappointment.

As the 1950s progressed, his huge workload meant that Pei had to delegate design responsibility to his now large architectural team, as he assumed an increasingly executive role. It could be argued that the nature of the Webb & Knapp work would not have allowed much in the way of cutting-edge design in any case. There were housing projects, as at Kips Bay on Manhattan's East Side, University Gardens in Chicago, and the Society Hill redevelopment in Philadelphia, which included the rehabilitation of eighteenth-century buildings and a mix of low-rise brick townhouses and high-rise concrete flats, all begun in 1956-57. Even where Pei accepted a commission on his own, as with the Green Earth Sciences building at MIT, there is still a feeling of constraint, even if it is self-imposed. The results were not always successful, either. The Green building, as well as having a standard Modernist-block appearance, suffered from a standard Modernist defect – vulnerability to the effects of wind.

By 1960 the difficulties which for some time had been afflicting Zeckendorf, who had overstretched himself financially, became acute, and Pei had no choice but to take an amicable leave of his employer and set up his own practice with the Webb & Knapp team of architects. Pei's career up to this time had been somewhat lopsided. On the one hand he had a huge team working for him and had been in charge of projects costing hundreds of millions of dollars; he had developed great skills as a manager and had got certain con-

structional techniques, such as poured-in-place concrete, down to a fine art. On the other hand, he had yet to design a major building of real originality and, because of his long association with a property developer, his name did not tend to be on anybody's short list for the sort of prestigious project that gets noticed in the architectural journals or in the drawing rooms of Park Avenue.

Things were not looking good for I. M. Pei and Associates; work, prestigious or otherwise, was thin on the ground; when a savior appeared in the unlikely person of the astronomer Walter Orr Roberts. Roberts ran the High Altitude Observatory at the University of Colorado, Boulder, and for years he had dreamt of building a laboratory on the mesa, or sandstone outcrop (a sort of American Ayer's Rock), above Boulder. The dream became a reality in 1960, when he accepted the directorship of the University Committee for Atmospheric Research on condition that he could build his research center on Table Mesa. The choice of an architect focused on finding someone relatively unknown and untested – which, in design terms, Pei was. Clearly Pei impressed the selection committee that he had the qualities of open-mindedness and dedication to grow with what was a demanding project, for in fall 1961 he was chosen.

The task was quite daunting. Roberts wanted his building to reflect the fact that atmospheric research (now such a hot topic) was a serious and vibrant science, while its layout had to encourage the chance encounters among its staff he felt were most productive to scientific endeavor, by not being too rigidly planned or hierarchical. Yet it also had to provide small private areas for discussion, flexibility for future changes of use in the form of movable walls, and maximum

wall space for bookshelves and blackboards. Added to all this was the problem of the uniquely sensitive site.

Pei's first design was a disappointment to Roberts, who felt it was 'just a bunch of towers'. Somewhat disheartened, Pei returned to the drawing board. His final design did not dispense entirely with the towers; instead he combined

three clusters of towers with lower-rise ranges, each part integrated into the next like an ingenious set of Chinese puzzle boxes. The planning provided all the variety and incident Roberts had wanted, and the concrete was colored with sand made from the stone of the mesa to blend into the landscape. The grass and flowers outside came right up to the door, and the approach road meandered up the mesa, further emphasizing the integration of building with landscape which had so impressed Pei when he looked at local pueblo buildings. Roberts was delighted and remained a lifelong friend of Pei's.

If Pei recognized shortcomings in the design – maybe the planning was just a bit too random – he also saw what cannot be denied, that it was a turning-point in his development as a designer. It certainly equipped him to take on what must have been the archetype of those prestigious projects which had eluded him while he was hitched to Zeckendorf, the design for the John F. Kennedy Memorial Library. In fact, the years with Webb & Knapp were probably more use to Pei in coping with what turned out to be the most long-drawn-out and frustrating project of his career, but he was not to know that in 1964.

Long before his assassination, John F. Kennedy had been planning a library. There was a precedent for a presidential

library in the form of the Franklin D. Roosevelt Library, but Kennedy, as well as an archive for his own books and papers, wanted to include a center for the study of politics and government, to encourage the young (he had been the

11

LEFT: Pei in 1981 with Jackie Kennedy Onassis, after receiving the National Art Club's Gold Medal of Honor. He had been her personal choice as architect of the Kennedy Library 15 years earlier.

RIGHT: Pei's first design for the Kennedy Library, on its original site adjacent to Harvard University, included a truncated glass pyramid.

BELOW RIGHT: The final design for the library, on a new site in Boston Harbor, features a complex combination of geometric forms.

youngest-ever President) to become involved in the country's administration. In October 1963 he chose the site, near Harvard University on the Charles River.

Kennedy's killing only a month later gave added impetus to the project. Now it was to be a memorial to him, in addition to the other roles he had determined for it. A building of such significance required careful consideration by the best-informed people of the day. A series of meetings was held, in Kennedy-clan homes and in Boston, of an advisory committee that, as well as the Kennedys and their advisors, included an international panel of architects such as Louis Kahn, Mies van der Rohe, Hideo Sasaki and I. M. Pei. A meeting was held in the Ritz-Carlton Hotel in Boston which also included Basil Spence, Lucio Costa, Alvar Aalto and Kenzo Tange, a truly glittering array of architectural talent. After an election procedure, which involved each of the architects having to nominate one of the others, a selection meeting of the 'winners' was held by Mrs Kennedy and the rest of the family at their Hyannisport home, followed by a series of interviews in the architects' offices.

Pei, who apart from the NCAR had done mainly property development, was up against the finest and best-known architects in the world. Yet it was a very personal decision in the end on Mrs Kennedy's part, despite the endless committee meetings. 'He didn't seem to have just one way to solve a problem. He seemed to approach each commission thinking only of it and then develop a way to make something beautiful.' Pei's appointment was finally announced to

the world at a press conference on 14 December 1964. There Bobby Kennedy wished him 'Good luck, Mr Pei!' He was going to need it, along with the patience of Job, and those years with Zeckendorf were to serve him well in this respect.

Part of the problem was the site. The one chosen by Kennedy himself was then occupied by a railroad marshaling yard. Even before he died, acquiring this site had proved problematic, and Harvard had offered a site diagonally across the Charles River at Brighton, next to Harvard Business School. With Kennedy's death and the expansion of the library to become a memorial to him, it became apparent that this site was inadequate for a project of this scale and once more the marshaling yard became first option. But time was a major problem; the railroad needed five years to evacuate the site, for a start. More important, however, was the change in the economic and political climate that took place while the project was delayed. The aura of hope, the sense of a new beginning, which characterized the Camelot era of Kennedy's presidency and the immediate aftermath had evaporated by the late 1960s. Bobby Kennedy had been assassinated, inflation was worse than at any time since the Korean war, and President Kennedy's elite force, the Green Berets, was now associated with the distinctly un-American slaughter at My Lai.

Faced with interminable interference and bureaucracy, Pei did not unveil his first design for the Kennedy Library until May 1973. It was an altogether more resolved design than what finally got built, and contained what have since

become two leitmotifs of Pei's architectural design — interlocking geometric forms and, even more famously, a glass pyramid, though in this case a truncated one. Mrs Kennedy approved of the design, but by this time the citizens of Cambridge were restless. The academics resented the fact that various departments were going to be hived off to supplement the Kennedy School of Government. The university authorities worried that the library, which was now also to

contain a museum, would be a tourist attraction and put too much of a strain on an area that was already 'traffic-sensitive'.

In desperation Pei came up with a smaller alternative design, without the pyramid. It was to no avail. The mounting difficulties wore away at the library committee to such an extent that in February 1975 they announced they would not build the library in Cambridge. Various alternative sites were immediately suggested and offered, from Washington DC, to Hyannisport, to Charlestown. Finally they all agreed on a site offered in Boston by a humbler institution, the University of Massachusetts, at Columbia Point in Boston Harbor, eight miles from the original site

Pei took full advantage of the site, persuading the donors to let him build right at the end of the point so the building would enjoy the optimum river views. He returned to a version of his original intersecting triangles plan, though the pyramid had gone, or, rather, been put into abeyance. The building was finally dedicated on 20 October 1979. The inscription on the wall of the atrium, taken from Kennedy's inaugural address, could hardly have been more apposite for the saga that had been the building of his memorial library.

All this will not be finished in the first one hundred days. Nor will it be finished in the first one thousand days, nor in the life of this Administration, nor even perhaps in our lifetime on this planet. But let us begin.

ABOVE: Dallas Municipal Administration Center with Henry Moore's *Three Piece Sculpture: Vertebrae*. Pei insisted on the plaza in front of the building to separate it from the rundown area that adjoined the site.

RIGHT: The East Building that Pei designed for the National Gallery of Art, Washington, was a brilliant solution to a problem site.

Fifteen years is a long time in an architect's career. The Kennedy commission had been a burden and a blessing for Pei. The main advantage for him was, of course, that it rocketed him to national, even international, prominence. And that naturally opened the door to the sort of large-scale, public or politically sensitive commissions that had eluded him while he had been tainted with the property developer's association. He was already building up a slate of prestigious clients by the time the Kennedy commission was announced. Some of his works from the early 1960s include the Newhouse Communications Center at Syracuse University, New York (1961-64), the Everson Museum of Art, also at Syracuse (1961-68), the TWA Terminal at JFK International Airport, New York (1962-70), the Wilmington Tower in Delaware (1963-71), and the extension to the Des Moines Art Center (1966-68). The art museum commissions would, of course, stand him in good stead for the future.

Another major project which ran alongside the Kennedy Library chronologically was, ironically, the Dallas Municipal

Administration Center. Dallas was deeply conscious of the reputation it had suddenly, with Kennedy's assassination there in November 1963, acquired in the world's eyes as a 'city of hate'. The mayor from January 1964, Eric Jonsson, was determined to make amends for the city in some way, and set up an ongoing project called 'Goals for Dallas'. A new city hall was felt to be one of these.

The choice of Pei as architect seems not to have been made because of the Kennedy Library, however. It probably had more to do with the friendship of Eric Jonsson with Cecil Green, who was the patron of Pei's Earth Sciences building at MIT. Incredibly, perhaps, Pei did not even realize that the city hall was the direct result of the city's feelings about the assassination, as he was unsure whether the decision to build it had been taken before or after the assassination. In a way, perhaps, ignorance was bliss in this case, as the project did not suffer the same burdens of association for him as the Kennedy Library.

Pei's appointment was made in February 1966, when he was still relatively unproven for such a major job. What impressed Jonsson and his colleagues, as it had impressed Mrs Kennedy before them, was Pei's dedication to the job in hand, and sensitivity to the particularities of the commission, especially to the site. He said a building should appear to grow naturally from its site, which required a careful choice of materials. He made it his business to get to know Dallas, a habit acquired in his Zeckendorf days, and his enthusiasm persuaded Jonsson to extend the site allocated for the build-

ing. Pei was dismayed by the unpromising acres of run-down housing and warehousing that separated the city-hall site from Dallas's burgeoning business district, and fought for a plaza in front of the city hall to provide a buffer zone to this area. As usual his personal brand of polite insistence won the day. The city authorities bought up a large area and earmarked it for a library; a parking lot under the plaza did much to offset the additional costs and ease traffic congestion.

The most striking thing about the design that Pei came up with for the city hall was that it was much wider at the top than the bottom and appeared to lean forward, supported, apparently, on three vast columns. It was, however, only eight storys high. This was because Pei conceived of the building as a visual counterpoint to the skyscrapers of the newly flourishing business district, to which the city hall 'points' across the plaza. The design provoked a certain amount of controversy and mirth, with some commentators predicting that the building would fall over into the plaza before it was completed.

Like most vast municipal projects, Dallas City Hall was beset by delays and problems, largely because of inflation, and it was not completed until 1977 – almost as late as the Kennedy Library. Technically it was a triumph, with Pei refining his poured-in-place concrete technique to create an almost seamless surface finish. With the public it was a success, the concrete being colored with local buff-colored sand to give it a less brutal and more natural appearance. A

testimony to its success with the client city was Pei's invitation many years later to design the Meyerson Symphony Center in Dallas.

I. M. Pei and Partners were riding the crest of a wave in the late 1960s, when a commission became available of even greater national significance than the Kennedy Library. The National Gallery of Art in Washington had been opened in 1941. Paid for entirely by Andrew Mellon, it was a monumental classical building designed by John Russell Pope in a style more reminiscent of 1841 than 1941. By the mid-1960s the museum was swiftly running out not only of exhibition space, but also of space for support services, such as conservation, and for study. The need to extend was made all the more pressing because the available site might otherwise be used for another purpose.

The major figure in all decisions made about the National Gallery East Building was Paul Mellon, Andrew Mellon's son. Paul Mellon had already used part of his vast personal fortune to build up an art collection especially rich in French Impressionists and eighteenth-century British art. He had also funded, or was to fund, six other art or educational establishments at Yale and Choate Rosemary Hall. In 1968 he agreed to fund half the cost of the East Building and his sister, Ailsa Mellon Bruce, agreed to provide the rest. The National Gallery's director, John Walker, estimated that the extension would cost $20 million. In the end it cost $95 million.

Another major influence in shaping the nature of the East Building was the director designate, J. Carter Brown, like Mellon a patrician American who mixed connoisseurship with business acumen. He was keen that the building should serve equally well, and reflect, the twin functions of exhibition space and study center. With his day-to-day involvement in the art world, Brown did not need to draw up and review a long list of potential architects. He knew it was between Pei, Louis Kahn and Philip Johnson. The final choice rested, of course, with Paul Mellon. Visits to Pei's Everson Museum of Art at Syracuse, and his additions to Saarinen's Des Moines Art Center, convinced them that Pei knew how to design an art gallery. What clinched it for Mellon, however, was the National Center for Atmospheric Research. He was very taken with the integration of the building into the site, the attention to detail in the interior, and, above all, the enthusiasm of the scientists who worked there for the building. One condition that Pei had to meet once he had been chosen was to take full personal control for design and supervision. This he was happy to do and it perhaps partly accounts for the building's success. The particular requirements of the commission were also very demanding. The National Gallery received vast numbers of visitors and it was anticipated – correctly – that the 'Beaubourg' effect (the 'exhibit' value of the building itself generating an increase in visitors) would come into play with the East Building.

The other great design problem was the shape of the site. Washington's street layout derives from L'Enfant's 1791 plan, which combines a rectilinear grid, concentric circles and radiating lines. The site for the East Building was affected by all these, being a right-angled triangle with a curved section sliced off one end. Pei's solution, reflecting the site and harking back to his first design for the Kennedy Library, was two interlocking triangles, one isosceles, one right-angled. It was a brilliant solution to the problem of relating the building to the National Gallery main building, while making optimum use of the odd site. The two separated but interlocked parts of the building also fulfilled the very different requirements of exhibition space and study center.

The East Building was a real technical challenge to Pei, in that the building committee required that it be built of the same Tennessee marble as the main building, whereas Pei had built only in concrete before. In fact, it would have been prohibitively expensive, even for Mellon's deep pocket, to use blocks of marble, and the East Building is constructed with concrete faced in three-inch thick sheets of marble from the same quarry as the original building. But the sense of crafting in the building can be seen at the sharp 19-degree corner, where instead of mitering the slabs together, Pei designed them so that they wrapped around the corner, creating the illusion that the building is of solid marble. Even inside, the exposed concrete is colored with powdered Tennessee-marble dust to create a chromatic harmony with the outside of the building.

The East Building was opened on 30 May 1978 to worldwide attention. By and large the reception was ecstatic. Some of the more rarefied architectural journals were a bit sniffy, complaining that the design was insufficiently daring or that Pei was trying to please all of the people all of the time. A comment he had made, that he had been designing for a 'mob scene. We needed to make the visit a pleasant one, so we built a circus' came back to haunt Pei. But the 15 years since the building opened have proved Pei's instincts

right, and it remains usable and accessible for curators and public alike.

For all that these major projects were gradually establishing I. M. Pei and Partners as a world-ranking firm, the practice was not immune from setbacks. A case in point was the John Hancock Tower in Boston, designed by Pei's chief associate, Henry Cobb. This behemoth, 60 storys and 790 ft high, clad in reflective glass and sited on Boston's historic Copley Square, is one of the last great Modernist skyscrapers. And it nearly ruined the Pei firm.

In 1966 Pei was commissioned by the John Hancock Mutual Insurance Company to build a new headquarters to rival the recently built Prudential Insurance Company building nearby. Pei's first design was for a cylindrical, masonry structure with two low-rise structures attached. This proved unworkable when Hancock suddenly decided they needed 30,000 not 22,000 sq ft of office space. Pei handed the project over to Henry Cobb, a foretaste of the future, looser association of Pei's partners. It was Cobb who came up with the slim, elegant skyscraper. But it was the whole firm which suffered when the huge panels of glass cladding began to crack during construction, in January 1973, and had to be replaced temporarily with plywood sheets.

The consequent jokes that the Hancock Tower was the world's tallest wooden building were the least of Pei and Partners' problems. A series of court actions followed, with Hancock suing Pei, Pei suing the glass-suppliers and the glass-suppliers counter-suing. It was all resolved out of court in 1981, with all the parties bound to secrecy over the outcome. But for the success of the National Gallery East Wing, the Hancock saga might have irrevocably damaged Pei's reputation in America. It certainly helps account for the

ABOVE LEFT: The Jacob K. Javits Convention Center in New York was designed as a monumental piece of civic sculpture, a twentieth-century 'crystal palace'.

RIGHT: Pei with the full-size mock-up of the main Louvre pyramid which he erected in the Cour Napoléon, in order to disarm critics of his Grand Louvre scheme.

firm's increasingly international outlook from the mid-1970s.

Apart from the Luce Memorial Chapel in Taiwan of 1954-63, Pei's practice had been almost exclusively North American up to the early 1970s. The Oversea-Chinese Banking Corporation Centre (1970-76) and Raffles City (1973-86), both in Singapore, marked a widening of outlook for Pei. But the chance of a major commission in his native China was an unexpected pleasure for him when it came. In 1974 Pei had paid his first visit to China since he had left in 1935. The Chinese were keen to establish links with the West following Nixon's re-establishment of diplomatic connections with China in 1972. They were particularly keen for contact with expatriate Chinese. Pei was not much impressed with Chinese architecture since the Revolution, however, and did not scruple to criticize its 'slavish' following of Soviet-style architecture.

This reaction against the non-national character of modern Chinese architecture may help account for the rather startling – given Pei's architecture over the previous 30 years – character of the Fragrant Hill Hotel which Pei was commissioned to build in 1979. The Chinese government wanted to build a group of hotels in Beijing as part of a concerted effort to open the country to tourism. What they had in mind was a group of high-rise buildings, western-style skyscrapers, emblems of a 'new' China, near the Forbidden City. Pei was horrified. While he might have been happy to design or sanction skyscrapers in the United States, a country the major part of whose civilization is only two hundred years old, Pei was conscious of the terrible danger such buildings could do to the historic heart of Beijing.

It was a major task, but Pei managed to persuade the authorities to build instead on a site outside the capital. They also adopted a planning policy restricting building heights in the vicinity of the Forbidden City, perhaps partly in response to Pei's argument. The design that Pei came up with was quite different from what the authorities originally expected, or from anything he had designed before. Before starting work Pei revisited his family's former villa in Suzhou, and was reminded of the interplay of buildings and gardens which is so important to traditional Chinese architecture.

Like the NCAR, the Fragrant Hill Hotel is a construction integrated with its site, in this case a highly wooded former imperial hunting ground. The buildings themselves are low-rise, built around courtyards, some with small gardens, intricately interlocked. What startled those who knew Pei as a one-time Modernist were the allusive decorative features; the buildings are unmistakeably Chinese in character. Working with untrained Chinese workmen taxed Pei's patience to the limit, but the building was completed in under a year and was opened on 17 October 1979.

Back in the United States a major project in his adopted city of New York came Pei's way in 1979. This was for a large convention center in a run-down area of the city, at 11th Avenue and 34th Street. This proved to be another of those bureaucracy-stifled projects that have bedevilled Pei's career. It was also slightly unusual in that, although the design is largely that of one of Pei's senior associates, James Freed, Pei took managerial control of the project. His experience in the 1950s of coping with municipal red tape probably saved the enterprise. The bureaucracy and procrastination were truly staggering, with Pei having to attend meeting after meeting with endless different officials. The budget was constantly cut and delays dragged on and on. In the end the building took seven years to complete. This was unreasonable, even given the fact that it covered 1.7 million sq ft, had a unique space-frame construction, and was high enough to accommodate the Statue of Liberty. But in the end the building was a success and it sits like a Crystal Palace in an otherwise unprepossessing district of New York.

By this time Pei was already thoroughly immersed in the project that has guaranteed him a place in the history books. In 1981 François Mitterand was elected President of France, after a very closely fought election with the then President, Valéry Giscard d'Estaing. As part of his vision for an active role for the government in redefining France's national and international standing, Mitterand planned a number of grand projets, which in Paris included the business district of La Défense, especially the grande Arche de la Défense, a sort of Arc de Triomphe for the late twentieth century. Another obvious candidate for restoration and redevelopment of some sort was the Louvre.

By 1981 the Louvre was a national disgrace in France. The museum's collection was so vast that nearly all the building had to be devoted to exhibiting and storing the collections. As a result support services for curators and conservators were squeezed into spaces that would have been inadequate for a provincial museum. Moreover the building's courtyards had become glorified car parks, and one whole wing, the Richelieu Wing to the north abutting the rue de Rivoli, was occupied by the Finance Ministry. Mitterand, with encouragement from his Minister of Culture, Jack Lang, decided that the Richelieu Wing must be returned to the museum. In so doing, however, the whole organization of the museum would be thrown into even further disarray. The problem was that there was only one major entrance into the Louvre, through the eastern facade. With an L-shaped building this made circulation awkward; with the addition of the Richelieu Wing making the building U-shaped, such an arrangement would be unworkable.

Any alteration to the Louvre was a political and cultural hot potato of the first order. The Louvre was not just a national art museum; its buildings were an architectural embodiment of France's history, and its turbulent transformation from monarchy to republic. The foundations of the Louvre dated back to the twelfth century, when it had been created as a royal fortress, and it had grown over the years into, successively, royal residence, imperial residence under

Napoleon, barracks, prison, administrative center and school of art. Its role as a gallery dated back to the late eighteenth century, when the Convention used it to display confiscated royal collections to the people. You tinkered with the Louvre at your peril, as architects as far back as the seventeenth century had discovered to their cost.

But Mitterand was not to be put off, and he appointed a senior civil servant, Emile Biasini, to assess the project and find an architect. By this time Pei was not the callow unknown he had seemed when he was chosen to design the Kennedy Library, or even the East Building of the National Gallery, and he was already on Biasini's shortlist of possible architects. Pei met him in Paris, and on being told that he was being considered, told Biasini he did not have the time to take part in competitions. During a trip to New York, Biasini persuaded Pei to consider the project, and Pei agreed to spend time assessing the feasibility of what was bound to be a daunting task.

After several months visiting every part of the Louvre, Pei announced that the project could be done – indeed, that it should be done – and that he would take it on. He immediately set up an office within an office in New York and told only a few people what he was up to. The most surprising feature of what can only be described as a highly radical solution to the problem of entrance and circulation in the museum was that he seems to have hit on the crucial ideas at a very early stage.

Having the entrance in the center of the Cour Napoléon made absolute logical sense. From there three passages could fan out to the three main wings, allowing a diffusion of the vast crowds to different parts of the museum. Using the vast area of the courtyard also meant that a subterranean museum annex could be created to house all the facilities that had been so sorely lacking before, extending ideas Pei had worked out at the Washington East Building, a good proportion of which is underground.

But the feature that people always immediately think of in connection with Pei's Louvre are the pyramids. Pei's interest in the form dates back at least to the abortive first design for the Kennedy Library, but there were more compelling cultural and historical reasons for using a pyramid. Apart from the obvious gravitas that was lent by its associations with the pyramids of Ancient Egypt and Classical Rome, Pei was very taken with the geometric designs of the great French landscape architect Le Nôtre. The possibility of creating a building that was both a solid part of an urban landscape and, if it were clad in glass, by turns reflective and invisible depending on the conditions of light, was very attractive to Pei. Extending the geometric idea, he proposed three further smaller pyramids lighting the three subterranean access passages. When Pei unveiled his model to Biasini, he was enchanted and immediately gave the go-ahead.

Of course, it was not that simple. This was the most politically sensitive project Pei had – or probably ever will have – to deal with. The decision was not just down to Biasini or, indeed, Mitterand, who was equally enthusiastic when he saw the model. The first sign of real trouble was when André Chabaud, the Louvre's Director, resigned in anticipation of the disruption which the scheme would cause to the museum. This was as nothing compared to a meeting of 23 January 1984, when Pei presented the scheme to the Commission Supérieure des Monuments Historiques, which had advisory powers only. The reception was extremely hostile and included commission members, who were supposedly seeing the plans for the first time, reading out prepared speeches of protest. There were also, unexpectedly, hostile members of the press present. The committee passed a unanimous vote of no confidence in the design.

Perhaps this response, which was reflected in the tone of newspaper and journal articles of the time as well as public opinion polls regarding the scheme (the great majority of which were unfavorable), should be seen in the context of some of the unfortunate modern buildings erected in Paris in the 1970s and early 1980s: the monolithic Montparnasse tower, the faceless office blocks of La Défense, and the replacement of the picturesque Les Halles with a frivolous Postmodern confection. But it is no excuse for the zenophobic, sometimes racist, tone of some of the attacks.

Pei was taken aback by the vehemence of the response, but was not discouraged. He set about marshaling his supporters, who included many significant and influential men and women from the worlds of the arts and politics. To start with he presented his scheme to the seven senior curators at the Louvre, who, after all, were most closely concerned with the building's real purpose, and secured their unanimous support. Additionally he had the highly vocal support of the composer Pierre Boulez and Mme Claude Pompidou, widow of the former President for whom another great architectural icon in Paris is named.

The real turning-point came in spring 1985, however, when Pei erected a full-size frame on the site as a mock-up of the main pyramid. Because the pyramid was to be of glass, Pei argued that the frame was a fair representation of the effect the pyramid would have on the Cour Napoléon. This was somewhat disingenuous as, of course, the glass would reflect as well as being transparent, and the framework would of necessity be heavier than the mock-up. But it served Pei's purpose admirably and, duly reassured, the tide of public opinion began to turn.

Ironically, it was at this more propitious moment that the project was most threatened by political changes. In 1986 Mitterand's socialists lost power to a conservative coalition;

a conservative minister, Edouard Balladur, came into office, and decided that the Finance Ministry wished to stay in its central Paris location. By this time, however, the Cour Napoléon part of the scheme was well under way, and by April 1986 the whole of the excavations had been completed. Mitterand re-established his position and in January 1988, with the prospect of the socialists' return to power in May, Balladur agreed to vacate the offices by the end of the year.

By that time the pyramids, which are the tip of the iceberg that is the huge new underground building, were complete. The building was opened to the public in spring 1989. A poll showed that a level of public condemnation of 90 percent only five years earlier had dropped to only 23 percent by 1989. And, in a statement made all the more significant by comparison with his pronouncements on the proposed addition to the National Gallery, London, Prince Charles, that barometer of the public's thoughts on the built environment, declared the building 'marvelous, very exciting'.

The litany of iconic projects which Pei masterminded should not blind one to the vast size – 300 employees – and complexity of Pei's practice by the late 1980s. By the time the Louvre Phase I (i.e. not the Richelieu Wing) was opened, I. M. Pei had designed more than 80 buildings or planning projects in his 40-year career, and the partnership had been involved in nearly twice that number, in North America, the Far East and Europe. But there is no denying that it is the icon buildings which have made the most of Pei's creative energies, and for which he will be remembered.

Three of these which ran simultaneously with the first phase of the Louvre were the Morton H. Meyerson Symphony Center in Dallas, the Creative Artists' Agency in Beverley Hills and the Choate Rosemary Hall Science Center in Wallingford, Connecticut, a triumvirate of buildings spanning the United States. The Meyerson Symphony Center was another project that taxed Pei's patience, and the funders' pockets, almost to breaking point. What saved the project in the end was Pei's tenacity and the fundraising skills of Texas businessman Ross Perot, who gained international recognition in 1992 as a presidential candidate. The building, when completed, was a major contribution to Dallas's Arts District. Its success, partly due to the work of acoustician Russell Johnson, helped put Dallas on the map as a classical concert venue. It also marked a major step forward in Pei's aesthetic, in that the purist geometry of his earlier buildings was softened into a more expressive, even baroque, sinuousness.

The one building above all others which has served to reaffirm Pei as an architect of world importance, however, proving that the Louvre was not just a 'one off', is the Bank of China building in Hong Kong. When Pei was approached by the Republic of China's representatives in 1982 to design a prestigious building in Hong Kong, in anticipation of Chinese resumption of control of the colony in 1997, the commission was not without personal difficulties for Pei. The Fragrant Hill Hotel was one thing; it was a tourist facility, not

RIGHT: Pei's Bank of China building combines a novel variation on the over-used skyscraper theme with great structural strength. Hong Kong is vulnerable to typhoons, and buildings have to meet wind-resistance standards twice as rigorous as those in New York.

a symbol of the Communist regime's economic might. Moreover Pei's father, who was still alive in 1982, had been a manager of the very same bank in Hong Kong in 1918, and he had been a bitter opponent of the Communists.

There were other difficulties as well. Pei, in spite of his public association with the Hancock Tower – which was, in any case, Cobb's project – had relatively little experience of building skyscrapers. And the site was so small, only 90,000 sq ft, that this was going to have to be a skyscraper. The other inauspicious association was that the site had been

used as a Japanese military headquarters during World War II, and prisoners had been tortured there.

On the positive side, there was the challenge to Pei of building a skyscraper to rival Norman Foster's high-tech 43-story Hongkong and Shanghai Banking Corporation headquarters, only two blocks away. What finally swayed Pei, perhaps, was the thought that the Bank of China building could serve as a symbol of rapprochement between the two Chinese peoples, and of hope for the future; a hope that was to be sadly overshadowed as the building was completed.

LEFT: The Bank of China building under construction. Most tall buildings are constructed like elongated steel boxes; where additional wind resistance is needed, steel is built into the sides to prevent the building being twisted out of true. Pei, with his engineering background, instead used a three-dimensional frame, a vastly enlarged version of a conventional truss, as the basic structure. The elements of this penetrate through the building, linking its four faces and allowing wind loads to be transferred to the four corners, which in turn are reinforced. Where the structural elements meet the glass skin, they are highlighted with aluminum cladding, creating the characteristic facade of superimposed boxed 'x'es.

Having accepted the commission, Pei was faced with the dilemma of finding a novel form for such an over-used (especially in Hong Kong) building type as the skyscraper. According to his son Sandi, Pei found the solution on a weekend trip to the family's villa at Katonah, while playing with some lengths of wood, fitting them together and experimenting with different lengths. Certainly the design he came up with suggests an interlocking of trapezoidal and triangular forms, a purist expression of his longstanding interest in geometrical shapes. At 70 storys high, the Bank of China building is the highest building in the world outside the United States. It was also a fortuitous design from a structural point of view. Hong Kong suffers from typhoons, and the buildings have to be highly wind-resistant. By making the whole building a form of giant truss, Pei achieved a much greater than usual structural strength.

In fact objections came not from the clients, or from the Hong Kong authorities, but from locals concerned at the building's apparently terrible *feng shui*. *Feng shui* is a traditional Chinese system for determining the most propitious way of building, from the choice of site, to the form of the building, and even to the orientation of the furniture. Hong Kong's *feng shui* experts were dismayed at Pei's design. Quite apart from the unfortunate associations of the site, there were twin radio masts on top of the tower. These apparently looked like the sticks of incense used to commemorate the dead. The highly visible cross-bracing also suggested death, in that condemned prisoners traditionally wore a name tag around their necks with a cross to suggest their imminent 'cancellation'.

All was resolved amicably when the Bank of China called in their own *feng shui* expert to advise. The mysticism of the skill means that an alternative explanation or assessment is usually possible. The building went up in record time, and cost only a fifth of what the Hongkong and Shanghai Bank cost. But as the building was nearing completion, Pei's expectations that it would become a symbol of reconciliation and hope were dashed by the massacre of student demonstrators in Tiananmen Square in Beijing. Pei expressed his outrage in an article in *The New York Times*, but it was a sad end all round to the saga.

The Bank of China is probably Pei's last 'big-statement' building. This is not a cause for sorrow, certainly not on his part, or a sign that he is retiring. Rather he is planning finally to take on those more personal projects which his large corporate practice has made virtually impossible since the Webb & Knapp days. Symptomatic of this was the announcement that the firm was now to be called Pei Cobb Freed and Partners, in recognition both of his senior partners' many years of work, and of the more detached role he now wants to take on. As he told his biographer, Carter Wiseman, in 1989: 'I no longer want to practice as I have. I want to enjoy life a bit more – and I want to do better work. I want to take on projects that were too small for the firm in the past.'

Pei has always succeeded, even when pressured by his clients, in resisting those extremes of architectural fashion, whether Modernism or Postmodernism, which have afflicted some of his prominent contemporaries. It will be interesting to see, now that he has allowed himself the luxury of developing it, what 'pure Pei' architecture will be like.

ABOVE RIGHT: Pei looks on as President Bush signs a proclamation declaring May 1990 to be Asian Pacific American Heritage Month.

RIGHT: Pei's design for the Barcelona Trade Center under construction.

The Development of an Architect, 1950-66

I.M.Pei is now reputedly a little shy about the buildings from his Webb & Knapp years. For an architect who now occupies a place near the zenith of the international architectural firmament, he certainly did spend a relatively long time as a property developer's 'house' architect. Some of Pei's largest projects for Webb & Knapp were not even strictly architectural, but were vast planning projects such as Roosevelt Field, New York (1951-56) and Washington Square East, Philadelphia (1957-59). In the case of Society Hill, also in Philadelphia (1957-64; page 27), Pei's solution was unusually conservation-minded for the 1950s and involved retaining most of the numerous eighteenth-century houses on the Delaware waterfront site. He added three high-rise blocks at one end of the site, arranged asymmetrically to minimize their impact on the area, and linked the elements by large and small public spaces and pools, in a manner that evokes his later, more personal 'Chinese puzzle' designs.

Inevitably, given the era and the type of work Pei was doing, the individual buildings of these years are dominated by what are now dismissed as 'concrete blocks'. These ranged from the Gulf Oil Building, Atlanta (1950-52; page 10), and the Mile High Center and Courthouse Square in Denver (1952-60; page 25), to public and private housing developments at Town Center Plaza, Washington DC (1953-61; page 26), University Gardens, Chicago (1956-61; page 26), and Kips Bay Plaza, New York (1957-62; page 11). What is immediately obvious is that in fact these are not all concrete (for instance, the Gulf Oil Building), nor are they all large-scale blocks (the University Gardens buildings are domestic-scale, two-story structures with brick infill panels).

Pei's large-scale work, when he set up his own office, is an organic growth from these projects, and represents an increasingly personal development of a broadly Modernist idiom. Even in the most uncompromisingly functionalist work such as the Green Earth Sciences building at MIT (1959-64; page 11) and the Wilmington office building in Delaware (1963-71; page 34) there are characteristic family resemblances, such as deepset windows and a refined 'artistry' to the composition of window and wall space.

Smaller, more personal commissions included Pei's very first commission, the futuristic additions to Webb & Knapp's own offices in New York (1950-51; page 10). Even more startling are two completely private commissions Pei undertook in the 1950s. One was for his own house at Katonah, New York (1951-52), an example of the most pared-down teutonic Modernism, with glass exterior walls and simple slab-concrete interior walls and roof. At the other end of the Modernist scale is the Luce Memorial Chapel at Taichung, Taiwan (1954-63), with its huge, soaring, steeply pitched, slightly concave roofs. The work of Le Corbusier is a leitmotiv in Pei's architecture up to the 1970s, as the comparison of Le Corbusier's monastery at La Tourette with Pei's Newhouse Communication Center at Syracuse University, New York (1961-64; page 28) clearly shows.

The turning-point in Pei's evolution as an architect was the National Center for Atmospheric Research (NCAR), Boulder, Colorado (1961-67; page 29-31). As we have already seen, the building owes much of its success to Pei's good understanding with his client, and to his response to the challenges of the site and the complexities of the building's uses. The John F. Kennedy Memorial Library (1964-79; pages 38, 39), on the other hand, was beset with difficulties. Despite Pei's extraordinary patience and tenacity in the face of all the changes to the brief, especially the 'movable' nature of the site, the building still has a feel of being 'over-designed', and obviously lacks the freshness of the NCAR, or, indeed of Pei's first design for the Kennedy Library itself (page 13).

Pei seems to have been particularly inspired in the mid-1960s by commissions for art galleries, notably the Everson Museum of Art at Syracuse, New York (1961-68; pages 32, 33) and his additions to the Des Moines Art Center (1966-68); pages 42-45. These are highly successful manipulations of geometric forms. In spite of the potentially forbidding and abstract nature of such an exercise, the buildings are highly functional as art galleries, with well-lighted spaces which progress logically and naturally, yet provide constant visual interest and surprises of vista. Most importantly, perhaps, they were a sound bedrock for one of Pei's finest works, the National Gallery East Building.

Mile High Center, Denver,
1952-56

ABOVE:
University Gardens,
housing and community development, Chicago,
1956-61

RIGHT ABOVE:
Society Hill,
residential complex, Philadelphia,
1957-64

RIGHT:
East-West Center,
Imin International Conference Center
at Jefferson Hall, Manoa, Hawaii, 1960-63:
the rear of the building, overlooking the Japanese garden

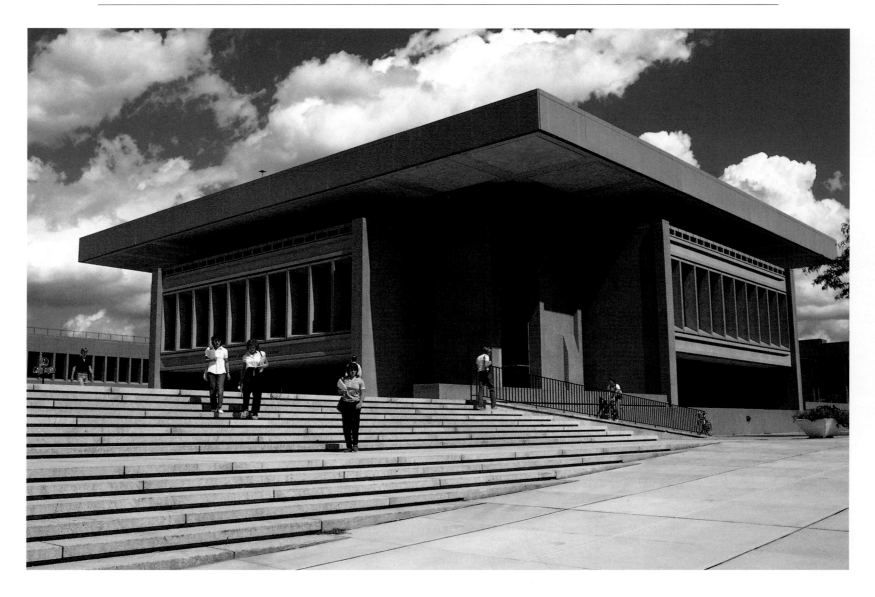

ABOVE:

S. I. Newhouse School of Public Communications,
Syracuse University, Syracuse, NY,
1961-64

RIGHT:

National Center for Atmospheric Research,
headquarters building, Boulder, Colorado,
1961-67

28

LEFT ABOVE:
The Mesa Laboratory,
National Center for Atmospheric Research,
Boulder, Colorado,
1961-67

LEFT:
Architectural detail of the laboratory showing the 400-acre nature preserve in which it is situated.

ABOVE:
Office and library space inside the laboratory.

Everson Museum of Art,
Syracuse, NY,
1961-68

Everson Museum of Art,
Syracuse, NY,
1961-68

Wilmington Tower,
office building, Wilmington, Delaware,
1963-71: the entrance area

Cleo Rogers Memorial County Library,
Columbus, Indiana,
1963-69

ABOVE:
Student quarters,
New College, Sarasota, Florida,
1963-67

RIGHT:
Reception area

John F. Kennedy Library,
Boston, 1964-79

John F. Kennedy Library,
Boston, 1964-79:
the lecture theater with its view of the Boston skyline

LEFT AND ABOVE:
Tandy House,
private residence, Fort Worth, Texas,
1965-69

LEFT AND ABOVE:
Des Moines Art Center,
Des Moines, Iowa,
1966-68

Des Moines Art Center,
Des Moines, Iowa,
1966-68

Des Moines Art Center,
Des Moines, Iowa,
1966-68

Acclaim in America
1966-77

Any architect who achieves both commercial success and critical and public acclaim is going to have buildings which stand out from his portfolio for reasons other than scale or profitability. Yet to imagine that these 'jewels in the crown' constitute the essence of an architect's achievement is to ignore a vast proportion of his output. Put simply, by the mid-1960s I. M. Pei was designing dozens of 'blockbuster' buildings, the type of commission that will ensure an architect a more than comfortable living. Large-scale commercial projects continued to come Pei's way, and Mies-inspired towers such as the Canadian Imperial Bank of Commerce in Toronto (1967-73; page 54) reveal that Pei was far from finished with Modernist paradigms.

The growth in overseas commissions began in the late 1960s. The phenomenal redevelopment of the tiny state of Singapore in south-east Asia provided Pei with the opportunity of realizing a twice-thwarted idea for a cylindrical skyscraper. In his early days with Zeckendorf he had designed a helical apartment tower (page 9), and this was revived in a more conventional version as the first design for the John Hancock Tower. Finally, at the Raffles City hotel and office building complex (1973-86; page 66), Pei was able to see it built.

The fact is that there were two 'jewels' in Pei's crown in this decade. The first of the two great projects which dominate this period was the Dallas City Hall (1966-77; pages 46-49). Although only fifteen years have passed since this building was completed, it now seems something of an architectural dinosaur; it is not just that it is built of concrete, now wholly out of fashion for public buildings, but it has a simplicity of form and purpose notably absent from such buildings today.

The East Building of the National Gallery of Art, Washington (1968-78; pages 56-59), although begun only two years after Dallas City Hall, belongs much more to the Pei of today, and is a far more complex and satisfying building than Dallas City Hall. This has partly to do with administrative differences in the commissions. Although Pei enjoyed a good relationship with Erik Jonsson, Dallas's mayor, the project was fraught with the same kind of creativity-numbing red tape as the John F. Kennedy Memorial Library. The National Gallery, by virtue of Paul Mellon's incalculable wealth, remained very much dominated by Mellon and J. Carter Brown, allowing Pei considerable freedom – not least relative freedom from worries about costs – to address the design problems.

The biggest problem was, of course, the awkwardness of the site. Because of the complexity of Washington's street plan, the site for the East Building is a right-angled triangle with the narrowest tip lopped off. Pei reputedly came up with the solution in a flash at a meeting and jotted it down on a scrap of paper. It was deceptively simple, deriving inspiration both from the geometry of the site and from Pei's taste for simple geometric shapes, and consisted of two contiguous triangles, one right-angled and one isosceles, with their long sides parallel to each other.

These two separate but integrated elements represent the dual but linked functions of the East Building: providing both exhibition space and a study and conservation center for art academics. The two parts interpenetrate at various points above and below ground. In the larger building, smaller diamond-shaped spaces are created by cutting off each corner at an angle, and some of these are further reduced to hexagonal-shaped rooms. The intricate interplay of large and small spaces is further enhanced by the use of walkways which, because of the unusual variety of angles in the whole building, provide ever-varied and surprising vistas.

Buildings with a cultural or scientific purpose seem always to bring out the best in I. M. Pei, and the East Building is the most prominent of a number of such buildings he designed in the late 1960s and early 1970s. The Fleishman building, NCAR (1966-68; page 50), was an extension to his own building for a valued client and represents a variation on a theme. The Herbert F. Johnson Museum of Art, at Cornell University (1968-73; page 55), on the other hand, was perhaps the last time he designed a truly Corbusian building. But the three buildings which are most closely linked with the East Building, and which perhaps point the way that Pei has developed since the late 1970s, are the Paul Mellon Center for the Arts, Choate Rosemary Hall (1968-72; pages 60-63), the Fine Arts Academic and Museum Building, Indiana University, Bloomington (1974-82; pages 68-69) and the Museum of Fine Arts, Boston, West Wing (1977-86; pages 70-73). Given these, his selection as the architect of the Louvre redevelopment can hardly be seen as the 'bolt from the blue' that it is sometimes represented in Europe.

Dallas Municipal Administration Center,
Dallas, Texas,
1966-77: interior

ABOVE:
Dallas Municipal Administration Center,
Dallas, Texas, 1966-77

RIGHT:
Detail of facade

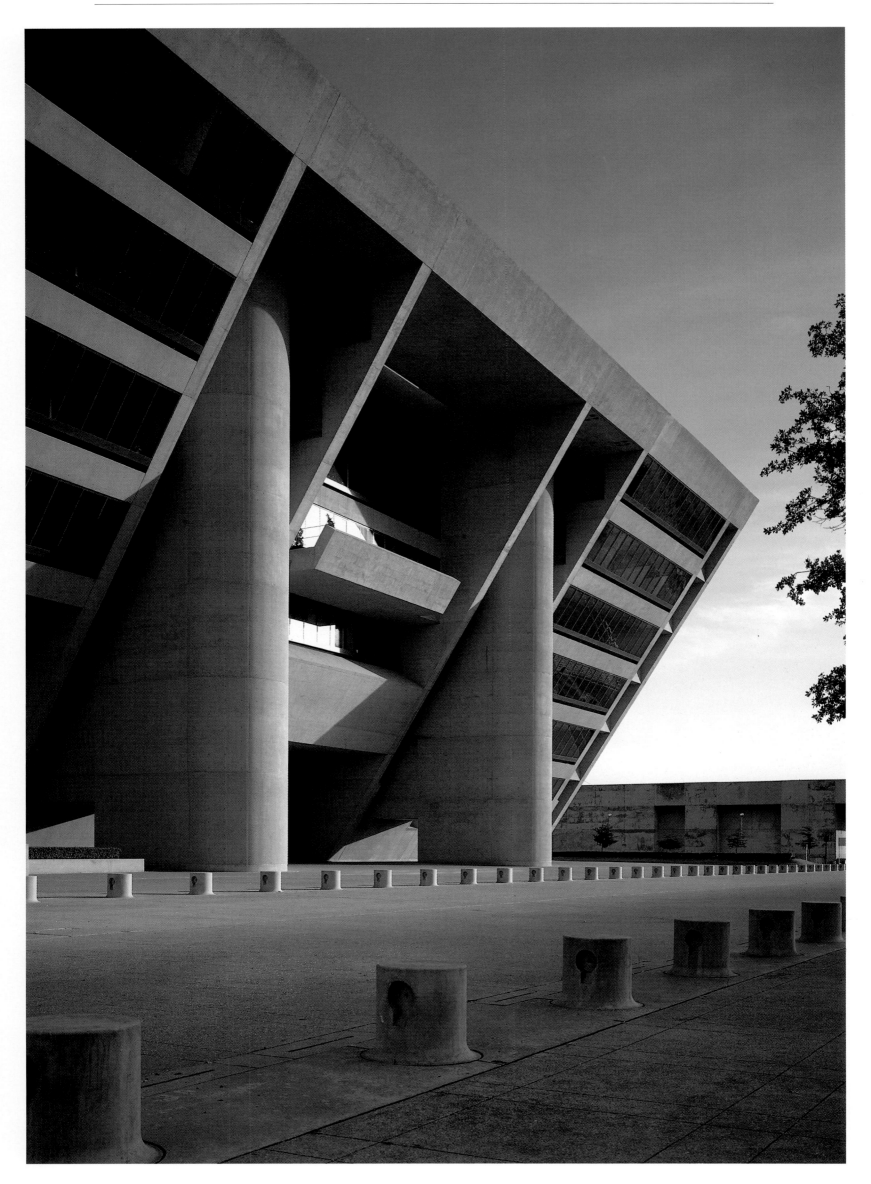

ABOVE:
Fleishmann Building,
National Center for Atmospheric Research,
Boulder, Colorado, 1966-68

RIGHT:
John Hancock Tower, Boston,
1966-76

50

LEFT:
Canadian Imperial Bank of Commerce, Toronto,
1967-73

ABOVE:
Herbert F. Johnson Museum of Art,
Cornell University, Ithaca, NY
1968-73

Paul Mellon Center for the Arts,
Choate Rosemary School, Wallingford, Connecticut,
1968-72

Paul Mellon Center for the Arts,
Choate Rosemary School, Wallingford, Connecticut,
1968-72

LEFT AND ABOVE:
Oversea-Chinese Banking Corporation Centre,
Singapore, 1970-76

LEFT:
Raffles Hotel,
Raffles City, Singapore,
1973-86

ABOVE:
Collyer Quay, Singapore,
1974-75

ABOVE AND RIGHT:
Fine Arts Academic and Museum Building,
Indiana University, Bloomington, Indiana,
1974-82

ABOVE AND RIGHT:
West Wing, Museum of Fine Arts, Boston,
1977-86

ABOVE AND RIGHT:
West Wing, Museum of Fine Arts, Boston,
1977-86

An International Reputation, 1978-94

The period since the late 1970s has seen a broadening of I. M. Pei's international commercial practice. Some of his buildings have been a development of the 'heroic' Modernist towers that he first designed at Webb & Knapp in the 1950s. In the years since the John Hancock Tower and despite the problems with that building, these have increasingly been glass-faced steel frames rather than reinforced concrete. The reflecting surface of such buildings is more in keeping with the more self-effacing — or at least less brutal — nature of late Modernism. Typical of these are the Sunning Plaza office and apartment complex in Hong Kong (1977-82), the Texas Commerce Center in Houston (1978-82; page 75), and the great canted-out twin Gateway Towers offices in Singapore (1981-90).

Even with purely commercial projects, there has been a move away from the previous uncompromising purity of form and an equally varied approach to materials, at least facing materials. This development can be traced from the IBM office building at Purchase, New York (1977-84; pages 76-77), through the Texas Commerce Center, Houston, to One Cabot Square, Canary Wharf, London (1990; page 104). These are basically steel-frame buildings, but variety is introduced in the form of varied heights within individual blocks, varied window and floor heights and, most obviously, traditional-look facing materials such as 'marble' or 'sandstone'.

What this suggests is that some time in the early 1980s I. M. Pei succumbed to Postmodernism. But is this true, or is it fair? One could easily choose a selection of buildings from his earliest days up to the present, such as his student project for a Shanghai art museum, the Gulf Oil Building, the Luce Memorial Chapel and the NCAR, and argue from them that, by virtue of the material or forms used or the way the building interacts with its site or reflects its cultural setting, Pei had always seen architecture too much as a cultural or personal expressive tool to be wholly a Modernist. Equally, if by Postmodernism one means brightly colored 'fun' classicism then Pei has yet to produce a Postmodernist design.

There is no doubt, however, that he has not been immune to the radical changes in the architectural *Zeitgeist* in the last 10 or 15 years. The turning point was, perhaps, the Fragrant Hill Hotel in Beijing (1979-82; pages 80, 81), with its low-built structure, obviously allusive plan of interlocking buildings, gardens and ponds, and simplified 'Chinese' decorative motifs. A similarly allusive quality is evident from this date in all Pei's buildings, even in skyscrapers such as the World Trade Center, Miami (1980-86) and the Regent Hotel, New York (1988-92; pages 102, 103), both of which have detailing recalling the great skyscrapers of the early twentieth century.

Such hints of America's architectural history can be read in the IBM entrance pavilion, Armonk, New York (1982-85; pages 92, 93), the Mount Sinai Hospital modernization and extension in New York (1983-90; pages 94, 95), the Los Angeles Creative Artists' Agency (1986-89; pages 100, 101), and the Kirklin Clinic (1992; page 105). But it should be stressed that these are only hints, not direct quotations, and they are specifically American. It is hard to imagine Pei designing anything like Philip Johnson's Chippendale-topped New York AT&T Building.

The multiplicity of readings possible with Pei's buildings of recent years can be seen especially at the Morton H Meyerson Symphony Center, Dallas (1981-89; pages 84-87) and the Science Center at Choate Rosemary Hall, Wallingford, Conn (1985-89; pages 96, 97). In both the proportion of window to wall is much less than in earlier buildings, and they have 'natural' finishes, formal sweeps of staircase and window. Is this then modern Classicism?

The quintessential rebuttal to those anxious to pigeonhole the Pei of the 1980s must be the Bank of China building in Hong Kong (1982-90; pages 88-91). Is it Modernist? But it is almost wilfully expressonist in its sculptural use of interlocking prisms. Is it then Postmodern? Yet it is completely without backward-looking allusion to either Chinese or western architectural traditions, and its 'giant truss' structure is a revolutionary solution to the problem of high-building stability in typhoon-prone Hong Kong. It is perhaps what a functionalist building looks like when the dogmas of Modernism have been discarded.

What the Pei building of the future will look like is another matter. Now that he has withdrawn from active leadership of Pei Cobb Freed, I. M. Pei is free to take on those more personal and idiosyncratic commissions which he has only occasionally allowed himself, although always with stimulating results, in the past. After a lifetime spent negotiating the narrow path between clients, builders, engineers, the press and the public, I. M. Pei has certainly earned the right to design things his way.

Texas Commerce Tower, Houston, Texas,
1974-82

IBM Building, Purchase, NY,
1977-84

Fragrant Hill Hotel, Beijing,
1979-82

Fragrant Hill Hotel, Beijing,
1979-82

Morton H. Meyerson Symphony Center,
Dallas, Texas, 1981-89

Morton H. Meyerson Symphony Center,
Dallas, Texas, 1981-89

Morton H. Meyerson Symphony Center,
Dallas, Texas, 1981-89

Bank of China, Hong Kong,
1982-90

LEFT AND ABOVE:
Bank of China, Hong Kong,
1982-90

Mount Sinai Hospital,
modernization and extension, New York,
1983-90

ABOVE AND RIGHT:
Choate Rosemary Hall Science Center,
Wallingford, Connecticut, 1985-89

LEFT AND ABOVE:
Choate Rosemary Hall Science Center,
Wallingford, Connecticut
1985-89

ABOVE AND RIGHT:
Creative Artists' Agency,
Beverley Hills, California,
1986-89

Four Seasons (originally Regent) Hotel,
New York, 1988-92

Four Seasons (originally Regent) Hotel,
New York, 1988-92

ABOVE AND RIGHT:
Kirklin Clinic, Birmingham, Alabama,
1989-92

LEFT:
One Cabot Square, Canary Wharf, London,
1991

The Louvre, Phases I-III, 1983-93

The redevelopment of the Louvre, which has been going on for more than ten years, was the first of François Mitterand's *grands projets* to be announced after he became President of France in 1981. While not a grand new building like, for instance, the Grande Arche de la Défense, the Louvre is the *grand projet* that the French public has taken to its heart, the one which will be Mitterand's memorial — so much so that he has been dubbed Mitteramses I, because of the public association of the project with the pyramidal shape.

The Louvre was not one building, but an accumulation of structures of diverse function. It had begun its existence as a fortress built against the English in the twelfth century, and was first opened as a public museum, displaying Louis XVI's collection, after the Revolution in 1793. The Louvre buildings as they were when Pei was employed opened out in a series of courtyards and wings stretching westward from the earliest surviving part, Pierre Lescot's mid-sixteenth-century Cour Carrée, toward the Tuileries Gardens and the Place de la Concorde beyond. The size of the site meant that, as the entrance was from the east, it was time-consuming and tiring to reach all parts of the museum. The net result was that most visitors did not bother; a survey before Pei's redesign revealed that the average length of a visit was just 80 minutes, less than half the time of the average visit to the Metropolitan Museum, New York.

Pei's decison to build a new entrance to the museum in the middle of the main courtyard, with three passages leading from it, was bold but logical; that point was roughly equidistant from the three main wings of the museum. The choice of the pyramid was also more rooted in tradition than its elemental shape might at first suggest. Certainly it conformed to Pei's longstanding taste for geometric forms, and specifically developed his thwarted first design for the Kennedy Library. But he has also acknowledged his debt to the designs of the seventeenth-century French landscape gardener Le Nôtre, and pyramidal designs are a particular feature of the work of eighteenth-century French architects such as Boullée, Le Canu and Neufforge. There is no doubt that it struck a chord with the French cultural consciousness.

Not least of Pei's problems in constructing the glass pyramid were technical ones. With the mockup of the pyramid, Pei had set himself the daunting task of creating a structure that would be virtually invisible. To achieve this, the French firm which was commissioned to supply the glass had to revive a technique for making pure, clear glass; most glass now has a slightly green tinge, due to iron oxide in its composition. The other structural challenge was the pyramid's frame. Put simply, should Pei use a few robust, or many fine, supporting members to achieve the desired impression of airiness? He opted for the latter, with the result that the main entrance pyramid is made up of 675 diamond-shaped and 118 trangular pieces of glass. The novelty of the design may be gauged from the fact that Pei had to employ techniques developed in competition yachting for the 'bowstring' tensioning system which holds the pyramid together.

The pyramid, and the vast network of grand entrance hall, passages and service rooms to which it provides access, were only Phase I of the Louvre redevelopment. Phases II and II included the creation of a huge underground shopping mall which stretches toward the Tuileries Gardens, a subterranean mirror of the courtyards stretching out above. This relationship is epitomized in the inverted glass pyramid which lights this part of the building, reaching, like a negative image of the entrance pyramid, from ceiling to floor.

The most significant part of Phases II and III, however, was the redesign of the Richelieu Wing. In fact 'wing' is rather a misleading term for a building which is larger than the British Museum, and roughly square with two internal courtyards. Pei's master stroke in tying the Richelieu Wing in with the rest of the Louvre was to roof the two internal courts, the Cour Marly and the Cour Puget, with glass pyramids which are a shallow echo of the entrance pyramid. These provide grand display spaces for monumental sculpture, including Louis XIV's *Horses of Marly*. The triumphant final gesture is the escalator, which provides striking views, through a vast circular window, of the pyramid and the courtyard below.

The Richelieu Wing was opened in November 1993, exactly 200 years after the Louvre was first opened as a public museum, but it is not the final phase. That will be Phase IV, which includes landscaping the northern end of the Louvre courtyard to provide a further visual and conceptual link between the Louvre, the Tuileries and the Place de la Concorde. Perhaps then, after 800 years, the Louvre will be truly complete.

The Grand Louvre, Phase I,
1983-89

ABOVE:
The Grand Louvre, Phase I,
the pyramids in the Cour Napoléon

RIGHT ABOVE:
The main pyramid giving access to the underground reception area

RIGHT BELOW:
The inverted pyramid in the underground reception area

LEFT ABOVE:
The Richelieu Wing

LEFT BELOW:
The Cour Marly

ABOVE:
The Cour Puget, given a glass roof by Pei

Acknowledgments

The publisher would like to thank designer Martin Bristow, picture researchers Sara E Dunphy and Suzanne O'Farrell, production manager Susan Brown and editor Jessica Hodge. We should also like to thank the following institutions, agencies and individuals for permission to reproduce illustrative material.

Robert Benson: pages 96, 97
André Biro: page 109 (above)
© Tom Bonner: page 105 (both)
Carlsten Associates: page 10 (above)
Courtesy Cornell University, Ithaca, NY, photo Bruce Wang: page 55
John Dowling: page 28
Courtesy East-West Center, Honolulu, HI, photo Deborah Booker: page 27 (below)
Final Focus: page 34
FPG International: pages 53, 64, 65, 75, 82
Owen Franken: pages 6, 107, 108, 109 (below), 110 (both), 111
Harvard University Graduate School of Design, Frances Loeb Library, Cambridge, MA: page 9 (left)
Indiana University Art Museum, Bloomington, IN: pages 68, 69
Balthasar Korab: pages 14, 15, 26, 27 (above), 35, 47, 48, 49, 54, 56, 57, 58, 59, 83

Ian Lambot: page 4-5
Nathaniel Lieberman/Four Seasons Hote: page 102
Life File: pages 23 (below)/photo Xavier Catalan; 66, 67/photos Emma Lee; 104/photo Andrew Ward
MIT Museum, Cambridge, MA: pages 8 (both), 11 (below)
Courtesy of Museum of Fine Arts, Boston: pages 70, 71
National Center for Atmospheric Research/University Corporation for Atmospheric Research/National Science Foundation: pages 29, 30 (both), 50
Courtesy New College, USF, at Sarasota, FL: pages 36, 37
Paul Mellon Center, Choate Rosemary School, Wallingford, CT: pages 60, 61, 62, 63
Reuters/Bettmann Newsphotos: pages 7, 17, 19, 21, 22
© Steve Rosenthal: pages 38, 39, 51, 52, 72, 73, 76-77, 78, 79, 92, 93, 98, 99
Ezra Stoller © Esto: pages 10 (below), 25, 31, 32, 33, 40, 41, 42, 43, 44, 45
Telegraph Colour Library, London: pages 80, 81
UPI/Bettmann Newsphotos: pages 9 (right), 11 (above), 12, 13 (both), 16, 23 (above)
Peter Vitale/Four Seasons Hotel, New York: page 103
© Paul Warchol: pages 1, 2, 84, 85, 86, 87, 88, 89, 90, 91, 94, 95, 100, 101